Ross is carrying groceries into the house. He lifts a sack of oranges and a sack of apples. Apples and oranges are about the same size. And his dad bought four of each.

Ross está entrando a la casa las bolsas de compras. Él levanta una bolsa de naranjas y una bolsa de manzanas. Las manzanas y naranjas son aproximadamente del mismo tamaño. Y su papá compró cuatro de cada una.

Why does the sack of oranges feel heavier?

¿Por qué la bolsa de naranja se siente más pesada?

Ross acted like a balance.

Ross actuó como una balanza.

He compared which fruit felt heavier. Using a real balance is another way to compare. On a balance, the heavier object dips down.

Él comparó cuál de las dos frutas se sentía más pesada. Usar una balanza real es otra manera de comparar. En una balanza el objeto más pesado baja.

Ross puts an apple and an orange on the balance. The side holding the orange dips down. The orange is heavier. That's why the sack of oranges felt heavier.

Ross coloca una manzana y una naranja en la balanza. El lado que sostiene a la naranja baja. La naranja es más pesada. Es por eso que la bolsa con naranjas se sentía más pesada.

This pepper is bigger than the apple.

Este pimiento es más grande que la manzana.

Which one will be heavier?

¿Cuál será más pesado?

The balance dips with the apple. The pepper is lighter than the apple.

La balanza baja con la manzana. El pimiento es más liviano que la manzana.

An object's size and how heavy it is are not the same.

El tamaño de un objeto y qué tan pesado es no son lo mismo.

A balance compares objects. But people have
made standard units to show an object's weight.

Weight is how heavy something is.

A weight can also be a pre-measured block.
Weight is measured in ounces, pounds, and tons.

16 ounces = 1 pound
2,000 pounds = 1 ton

Una balanza compara objetos. Pero la gente ha
fabricado unidades estándar para mostrar
el peso de un objeto.

El peso es qué tan pesado es algo.

Un peso también puede ser un bloque premedido.
El peso se mide en onzas, libras y toneladas.

16 onzas = 1 libra
2,000 libras = 1 tonelada

In the metric system, weight is measured in grams, kilograms, and metric tons.

1,000 grams = 1 kilogram
1,000 kilograms = 1 metric ton

In this book, we show the metric weight in parentheses after the other measurements.

En el sistema métrico el peso se mide en gramos, kilogramos y toneladas métricas.

1,000 gramos = 1 kilo
1,000 kilos = 1 tonelada métrica

En este libro, mostramos el peso métrico entre paréntesis después de las otras medidas.

Ross can use a balance as a scale.

Ross puede usar una balanza como una báscula.

Scales measure an object's weight.
How much does the apple weigh?

La báscula mide el peso del objeto.
¿Cuánto pesa la manzana?

Ross stacks gram weights on one side. He keeps stacking until the balance is even. Small objects are measured in ounces or grams. Big objects are measured in pounds or kilograms.

Ross apila pesas de gramos en un lado. Él sigue apilándolas hasta que la balanza se empareja. Los objetos pequeños se miden en onzas o gramos. Los objetos grandes se miden en libras o kilogramos.

The apple weighs 5 ounces (142 grams).

La manzana pesa 5 onzas (142 gramos).

Most scales don't need separate weights. Just put the object on the scale and read the number.

This orange weighs 9 ounces (255 g).

La naranja pesa 9 onzas (255 g).

La mayoría de las básculas no necesita pesas separadas. Sólo necesitas colocar el objeto en la báscula y leer el número.

Today Ross is back at the store for some candy. The candy is sold by the pound. Are there more mints in a pound or more caramels?

Hoy Ross volvió a la tienda para comprar caramelos. Los caramelos se venden por libra. ¿Hay más mentas en una libra que caramelos de leche?

Let's find out!
¡Vamos a averiguarlo!

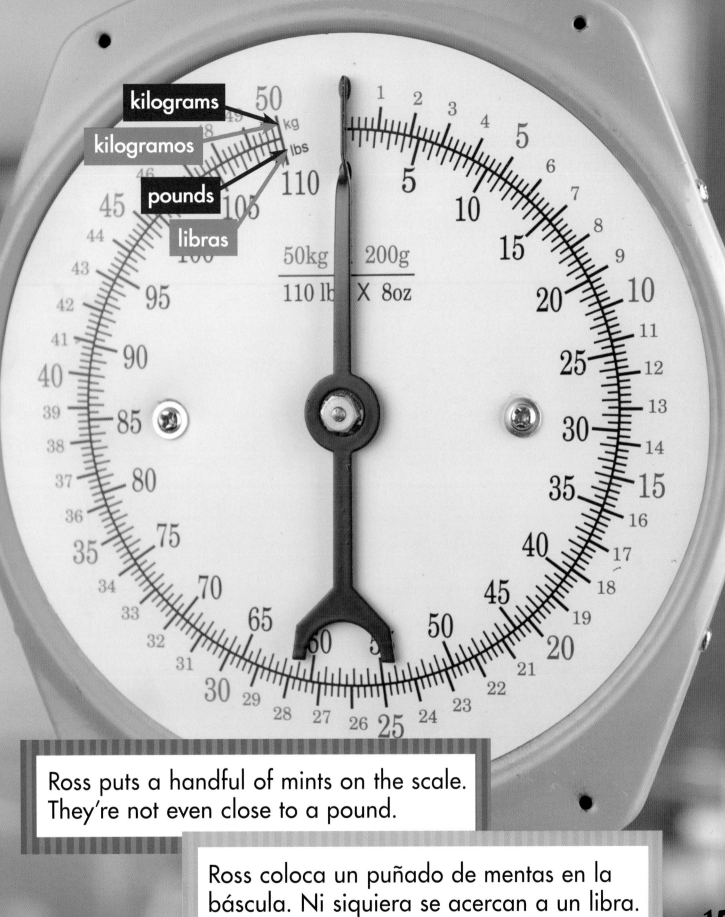

kilograms

kilogramos

pounds

libras

Ross puts a handful of mints on the scale. They're not even close to a pound.

Ross coloca un puñado de mentas en la báscula. Ni siquiera se acercan a un libra.

Ross adds more mints. **Wow!** It takes 90 mints to make the scale read 1 pound (0.45 kilogram).

Ross agrega más mentas. **¡Oh!** Se necesitan 90 mentas para hacer que la báscula lea 1 libra (0.45 kilogramos).

50kg X 200g

110 lbs X 8oz

It takes only
54 caramels to
get to 1 pound.

Se necesitan sólo
54 caramelos de
leche para llegar
a 1 libra.

One caramel is heavier
than one mint.

Un caramelo de leche es más
pesado que una menta.

Scales aren't just for the grocery store.

Las básculas no se usan sólo en la tiendas de comestibles.

You can use food scales on the kitchen counter. A slice of bread weighs 1 ounce (28 g).

TIME

°C°F

28

TARE/ON

UNIT

max:3000g d=1g

Tú puedes usar básculas de alimentos en la mesada de la cocina. Una rebanada de pan pesa 1 onza (28 g).

Sixteen ounces make 1 pound (454 g, or 0.45 kg). So 16 slices of bread weigh 1 pound.

Dieciséis onzas son 1 libra (454 g o 0.45 kg). Por lo tanto, 16 rebanadas de pan pesan 1 libra.

Some scales are for bigger things. This floor scale at the veterinarian's office weighs animals.

Duke weighs 138 pounds (62.6 kg)!

¡Duke pesa 138 libras (62.6 kg)!

Algunas básculas son para cosas más grandes. Esta báscula de piso en la oficina del veterinario pesa animales.

Princess weighs only 6.4 pounds (2.9 kg).

Princess pesa sólo 6.4 libras (2.9 kg).

Some places use very strong floor scales to measure tons. This warehouse is shipping more than 1,000 pounds, or ½ ton (0.45 metric ton) of books.

Algunos lugares usan básculas de piso muy fuertes para medir toneladas. Este depósito está enviando más de 1,000 libras, o ½ tonelada (0.45 tonelada métrica) de libros.

Grandpa keeps a fish scale in his tackle box.
Ross and his grandpa each caught a fish!
The fish hang from the scale to be weighed.

Abuelo mantiene una báscula para peces en su caja de pesca. ¡Ross y su abuelo pescaron cada uno un pez! El pez colgó de la báscula para ser pesado.

Whose fish is heavier?

¿Qué pescado es más pesado?

Ross' fish is 8 ounces (227 g).
Grandpa's fish is a little lighter.
His weighs 6 ounces (170 g).

El pescado de Ross pesa 8 onzas (227 g).
El pescado de Abuelo es un poquito más
liviano. Su pescado pesa 6 onzas (170 g).

Ross wonders how much he weighs compared to his big catch.

Ross se pregunta cuánto pesa él comparado con su pescado.

A bathroom scale measures a person's weight. Ross weighs 50 pounds (22.7 kg).

Una báscula de baño mide el peso de una persona. Ross pesa 50 libras (22.7 kg).

Can you imagine catching a 50-pound fish?

¿Puedes imaginarte pescar un pez de 50 libras?

Cool Measuring Facts
Datos divertidos sobre medir

a Chihuahua

un Chihuahua

• The **lightest dog** on record is a Chihuahua named Dancer. It weighs 1.1 pounds (0.5 kg).

• El **perro más liviano** registrado es un Chihuahua llamado Dancer. Él pesa 1.1 libras (0.5 kg).

• The world's **biggest animal** is the blue whale. The biggest one to be measured weighed 198 tons (180 metric tons) and was 97 feet (30 meters) long.

• El **animal más grande** del mundo es la ballena azul. La más grande que se ha medido pesó 198 toneladas (180 toneladas métricas) y tenía 97 pies (30 metros) de largo.

• The **largest apple** ever found weighed 4 pounds, 1 ounce (1.8 kg). It was picked in Japan.

• La **manzana más grande** que se encontró pesó 4 libras, 1 onza (1.8 kg). Se recolectó en Japón.

• The ostrich is the world's **heaviest bird**. Males weigh up to 287 pounds (130 kg). The bee hummingbird is the world's tiniest bird, weighing .07 ounces (2 g).

• El avestruz es el **ave más pesada** del mundo. Los machos pesan hasta 287 libras (130 kg). El colibrí abeja es el ave más pequeña del mundo y pesa 0.07 onzas (2 g).

• **Andy Bolton** holds the world record for lifting a weight. He lifted a 1,008.6-pound (457.5-kg) barbell from the floor and held it above his knees.

• **Andy Bolton** tiene el récord mundial de levantar una pesa. Él levantó una mancuerna de 1,008.6 libras (457.5 kg) del piso y la mantuvo arriba de sus rodillas.

Glossary

balance—a tool used to compare or measure weight; balances have a beam supported in the center with two equal pans on each end

measure—to find out the amount of something

metric system—a system of measurement based on counting by 10s; grams and kilograms are basic units of measuring weight in the metric system

ounce—a unit of weight equal to $1/16$ of a pound

pound—a unit of weight equal to 16 ounces

scale—a tool used to measure weight

ton—a unit of weight equal to 2,000 pounds

Internet Sites

FactHound offers a safe, fun way to find Internet sites related to this book. All of the sites on FactHound have been researched by our staff.

Here's all you do:

Visit *www.facthound.com*

Type in this code: 9781429668927

 Check out projects, games and lots more at
www.capstonekids.com

Glosario

la balanza—una herramienta que usa para comparar o medir pesos; la balanza tiene una viga sostenida en el medio con dos recipientes iguales en cada extremo

la báscula—una herramienta que se usa para medir pesos

la libra—una unidad de peso que equivale a 16 onzas

medir—averiguar la cantidad de algo

la onza—una unidad de peso que equivale a $^1/16$ de una libra

el sistema métrico—un sistema de medición basado en contar de a 10; gramos y kilogramos son unidades básicas de medir peso en el sistema métrico

la tonelada—una unidad de peso que equivale a 2,000 libras

Sitios de Internet

FactHound brinda una forma segura y divertida de encontrar sitios de Internet relacionados con este libro. Todos los sitios en FactHound han sido investigados por nuestro personal.

Esto es todo lo que tienes que hacer:

Visita *www.facthound.com*

Ingresa este código: 9781429668927

¡Algo súper divertido! Hay proyectos, juegos y mucho más en www.capstonekids.com

Index

Índice

A+ Books are published by Capstone Press,
1710 Roe Crest Drive, North Mankato, Minnesota 56003.
www.capstonepub.com

Library of Congress Cataloging-in-Publication Data
Adamson, Thomas K., 1970–
  [How do you measure weight? Spanish & English]
  ¿Cómo mides el peso? = How do you measure weight? / por
Thomas K. and Heather Adamson.
    p. cm.—(A+ bilingüe. Mídelo = A+ bilingual. Measure it)
  Summary: "Simple text and color photographs describe the
units and tools used to measure weight—in both English and
Spanish"—Provided by publisher.
  Includes index.
  ISBN 978-1-4296-6892-7 (library binding)
  1. Weights and measures—Juvenile literature. 2. Units of
measurement—Juvenile literature. I. Adamson, Heather, 1974– II.
Title. III. Title: How do you measure weight?
  QC90.6.A3318 2012
  530.8'1—dc22   2011001353

Credits
Gillia Olson, editor; Strictly Spanish, translation services;
  Juliette Peters, designer; Eric Manske, bilingual book designer;
  Sarah Schuette, photo studio specialist; Marcy Morin, studio
  scheduler; Laura Manthe, production specialist

Photo Credits
All photos by Capstone Studio/Karon Dubke

Note to Parents, Teachers, and Librarians
The Mídelo/Measure It series uses color photographs and a
nonfiction format to introduce readers to measuring concepts in
both English and Spanish. *¿Cómo mides el peso?/How Do You
Measure Weight?* is designed to be read aloud to a
pre-reader, or to be read independently by an early reader.
Images and narrative promote mathematical thinking by
showing that objects and time have measurable properties,
that comparisons such as longer or shorter can be made
between multiple objects and time-spans, and that there are
standard and non-standard units for measuring. The book
encourages further learning by including the following sections:
Cool Facts, Glossary, Internet Sites, and Index. Early readers may
need assistance using these features.

Printed in the United States of America at Corporate Graphics
in North Mankato, Minnesota.
102012   007006R